WHEN WOUNDS WON'T HEAL

George E. Vandeman

Pacific Press Publishing Association
Boise, Idaho
Montemorelos, Nuevo Leon, Mexico
Oshawa, Ontario, Canada

Edited by Ken McFarland
Cover by Tim Larson
Cover Art by Nery Cruz
Type set in 10/12 Century Schoolbook

Copyright © 1985 by
Pacific Press Publishing Association
Printed in United States of America
All Rights Reserved

Library of Congress Cataloging in Publication Data

Vandeman, George E.
  When wounds won't heal.

  1. Marriage—Religious aspects—Christianity. 2. Family—Religious life. I. Title.
BV834.V353   1985   248.8'4   85-25911
ISBN 0-8163-0632-X

Contents

When Wounds Won't Heal	5
Formula for Two	15
Trouble With the Personnel	28
Your Irreplaceable Role	40

When Wounds Won't Heal

Small children who fall and scrape their knees usually have Mommy nearby, ready with a band-aid and a kiss to make it all better. Teenagers enduring still another dateless Saturday night can count on a trusted friend to ease the lonely hours. And after marriage, most people find some way of coping with the occasional hurts and disappointments of adulthood.

But what about the wounds that band-aids and comforting words just don't reach? What about the emotional traumas that leave scars deep inside us? What do we do when wounds simply refuse to heal?

Three-year-old Lori is playing happily one day outside her home in a Denver suburb. A young man drives up, parks by the curb, and entices the child into his car. Moments later, Lori's mother notices that the child has disappeared. She begins to search, at first calmly, then frantically, for her missing daughter. The police are notified. They alert personnel all over the city. Lori has disappeared without a trace.

A few days pass. A group of bird watchers are hiking through a mountain park about forty minutes from Lori's home. Suddenly they stop on the trail—somewhere a child is crying. The hikers follow the faint cries to an outhouse. Opening the door, they look down into the pit and see something they will never forget. A child stands in the filth, shivering, almost naked. "What are you doing here?" they ask. "I'm home," little Lori replies. "I live here."

This innocent three-year-old had been sexually abused. Lori was reunited with her tearful parents—safe at last in her mother's arms. But the wound—the wound would remain.

Was Lori an isolated case? Unfortunately not. We live in a scar-intensive world. Children now must face terrible new facts of life.

Not long ago, the quiet, grandmotherly founder of a Los Angeles preschool was arrested. Authorities charged that she and other staff members had molested more than forty children over the course of a decade. For years the preschool staff had frightened their toddlers into silence by slaughtering small animals in front of them. But finally, with the help of trained counselors, a few of the children managed to tell their horror stories of intimidation and abuse.

Stories of molestation abound, and we learn to our shock that the criminal is often a relative or friend of the family, betraying the trust of an innocent child.

We hear unbelievable accounts of children brutalized by their parents, infants neglected, latch-key kids left to fend for themselves, adolescents kidnapped by pornographers, child prostitutes walking the streets of our great cities.

Ours is by all counts a scar-intensive world. Is it any wonder that so many suffer from damaged emotions?

And these are only the most sensational of the traumas that wound people so deeply. Most of us have had a less-than-perfect past, and many of us are burdened with some hidden scar—a secret wound that never quite heals.

Many things can scar. A parent who could never quite accept our performance—we were never quite good enough. Classmates who teased us unmercifully at some awkward, vulnerable age. A friend who betrayed us in an hour of need. An old sin that keeps gnawing away at our souls.

When traumas in our past produce emotional scars, our self-esteem is often damaged. We feel inadequate and try to make up for this lack in a number of unhealthy ways.

First, many of us try to hide from our scars. We try to ignore them and pretend that the wounds simply don't exist. It's so very hard to accept the fact that something terrible—something very unjust—has happened to us.

But scars, though hidden, still can hamper our lives. In running away from them, we get tangled up in emotional detours. Some begin to think, subconsciously, "I must have done something terrible to deserve such a tragedy." A twisted sense of guilt can develop, leading us to say, "No one could ever love me. Everything I do ends up wrong."

Hidden scars sometimes drive people toward a false perfectionism—always trying hard to be good enough, desperately trying to please others. But they never can seem to make it. They never feel good enough; they can never find rest.

Hidden scars can make people supersensitive. They once reached out for approval and love and were deeply wounded. Bearing that hurt inside makes them overly sensitive to further pain. Some walk around with their hearts on their sleeves; others cover up their sensitivity with tough exteriors. In either case, the real wound remains—hidden, unhealed, festering.

Hidden scars make people afraid. At some point in

the past they became victims. That experience convinced them that they really can't control what happens to them. And they remain victims. Fears force people to the sidelines. They watch life go by from behind the barrier of their hidden scars.

If you have been deeply wounded, you may feel that nothing can penetrate that barrier and that nothing can undo the emotional damage. You may well think that past traumas will haunt you always.

But I believe there is genuine healing available for the deepest wound. There is a way to deal with our damaged emotions, our wounded self-esteem. There are steps we can take, through God's grace, to gain control of our lives again. Our Lord wants us to be disciples, not simply victims.

First, we must deal with the problem squarely. We must be willing to come face to face with that hidden wound.

Ben had been cowering his way through life, always afraid of attempting anything, always afraid of offending someone. He spoke in a barely audible voice. Something was obviously holding him back. Help finally came at a marriage-enrichment retreat. Surrounded by loving, supporting Christians, he was able to share some painful memories.

When Ben was a boy, his mother had suffered a nervous breakdown. Shortly afterward he overheard the neighbors whispering. "You know why she had a breakdown," they said. "It's because of that little boy, following her around all the time, clinging to her apron strings."

Now that's a pretty heavy burden for a child to carry. Imagine hearing people say, "You are the cause of your mother's breakdown, of her being an invalid." All those years Ben had been doing inner penance for an unjust accusation. He was trying to make up for the terrible wrong he thought he had done.

But as Ben shared with this group, the burden was lifted. As he sobbed out his painful story, he experienced release and acceptance for the first time.

Ben had to face that hidden scar. He had to say, "Yes, it happened. Yes, it was terribly unfair, but I'm going to step through that false accusation; I'm going to say goodbye."

As we are enabled to face our hidden scars, we need to face something else too—our responsibility. Now let me explain. We are not responsible for the trauma in our past. We are not somehow guilty for being wounded. No. But we ARE responsible for our reaction to the hurt. We can take charge of our response.

Let me tell you about Josephine. This deeply troubled young woman insisted, to all her doctors, that she wasn't her father's daughter. She was absolutely certain of it. The records proved otherwise, but nothing could persuade Josephine.

Then a Christian physician began to counsel with her. He discovered that, years before, this woman had been mistreated by her father and had rebelled against his harshness. Gently this physician tried to lead her to a healthier response to her unfortunate past.

It was a hard struggle. Josephine had a difficult time accepting her father. But after much prayer and counsel, she came to realize that her denial only worsened the wounds. She discovered a new fellowship with God and was able to become reconciled to her father.

You see, we must decide whether we really want to recover from our wounds. Do we want to take charge of our response to the past? We must answer the question Jesus posed to the paralytic lying helplessly by the Pool of Bethesda: "Do you want to be healed?"

Jesus didn't ask, "Do you want to lie here and talk about your problem?" or, "Do you want to complain about how unfairly life has treated you?" The Saviour simply asked, "Do you want to be healed?"

Now we come to a very important step. As we accept responsibility for our response to a wound, we must learn to forgive those who have wounded us. And that's not easy. In fact, humanly speaking, it is often impossible.

All our lives we may have been trying to collect on a debt. Someone owes us for the terrible hurt we've experienced. Subconsciously we expect people to pay up.

A Christian scholar found himself reacting in a violent anger at the most unexpected times. He couldn't understand it. The man read the Scriptures, he prayed, but still couldn't quite get a handle on the problem.

Finally, he paid a visit to a Christian counselor. He began recalling incidents from childhood—grade-school sports—how clumsy he had been! Every recess was agony for him. The bigger boys bullied him around. Others made fun of his awkwardness.

Now, years later, those scenes were vivid in his mind. He could recall the faces and names of each of his tormentors. Evidently this was the root of his anger.

So the scholar was led through a simple exercise. He named each of those schoolmates and placed them under God's forgiveness: "I claim forgiveness for Jack, I claim forgiveness for Sally," and so on.

This was painful, but through his prayer the scholar found the grace to truly forgive, and slowly God healed those painful scars of the heart.

Jesus taught that we should forgive one another just as He has forgiven us. Christ forgives freely, without reservation. Forgiveness freely given opens up our hearts for healing.

Now we can bring our feelings to God. Our feelings of anger, humiliation, shame. Feelings we dared not share before. We can bring them to Him because He is the Wounded Healer.

He is the One who sobbed heart and soul out on the cold ground of Gethsemane. He is the One wounded for our trangressions and bruised for our iniquities, the One rejected by His own people, the One who endured mockery as He hung alone on the cross.

Whatever dark picture stains your memory, He will understand. He has seen darker still. Whatever painful trauma continues to haunt you, He can bear. He has born a greater pain.

Share that secret hurt with a heavenly Father, a Wounded Healer, who sympathizes with your weakness. As you share your pain, He will share His healing grace. And you will be able to accept His regard, His picture of who you really are. God has a lot to say about whom we really are.

Listen to the apostle John's exclamation: "How great is the love the Father has lavished on us, that we should be called children of God! And that is what we are!" 1 John 3:1, NIV.

Can you thank God that He has chosen you as His child? That fact must become real to you. Say it—express thanks to God that you are His chosen one. No matter how you may have been scarred in the past, now, today, your heavenly Father gives you a new identity.

Think of those scarred individuals in the Bible who received a new identity from their Lord. Jacob was known as the cheater, the man who had robbed his own brother of an inheritance. But God gave him a new identity. Jacob became Israel, the father of many nations.

David carried within him the wound of a terrible sin against Bathsheba and Uriah, her husband. But through repentance he found a new identity, as a man after God's own heart.

The thief on the cross bore many scars—his whole life wasted in crime, his heart filled with regret. But a word from the Saviour made him a new man and freed him from the horrible past. Now he was bound for Paradise.

Paul was once haunted by the faces of those he had so zealously persecuted. He had fought against Christ Himself. But one day on the road to Damascus, Jesus gave the persecutor a new identity—Paul, Apostle to the Gentiles.

This same Paul tells us that, as believers, we are "accepted in the Beloved." Ephesians 1:6, NKJV.

Do you recall another time when that word *beloved* was used in Scripture? At Christ's baptism, the Father said, "This is My beloved Son, in whom I am well pleased." Matthew 3:17, NKJV.

How the Father cherished His beloved Son. But listen, that is just how we are cherished. We are accepted in the Beloved. Even as we bare our ugliest scars, even as we reveal those dark, hidden emotions—we are accepted in the Beloved.

When we focus on that truth and claim it for ourselves, we will acquire a Christ-oriented self-image, and true inner healing can begin.

We may have been programmed to belittle ourselves. Our past may have shoved us into a narrow mold—old voices telling us we are not valued, not worth it. But God can reprogram those unhealthy thought patterns.

Listen to the good news of Romans 12:2, NIV: "Do not conform any longer to the pattern of this world, but be transformed by the renewing of your mind."

WHEN WOUNDS WON'T HEAL 13

When you catch yourself falling back into the old pattern, nursing the old wound, accepting that old feeling of worthlessness, *stop*. Claim God's promise to renew your mind. Focus on the new facts. You are chosen as the heavenly Father's child. You are accepted in the Beloved.

Several years ago Corrie ten Boom decided to visit her home town—the quiet little town of Haarlem. Corrie had been away only a few years, but those years—spent in a Nazi concentration camp—seemed like an eternity.

Late one evening she arrived at her old, familiar street. She walked down by the old, familiar houses. In the darkness, she peered through a window into the watchmaker's shop where her father had worked. She ran her hands along the door and listened in the dark.

Corrie remembered the voices of her sister and father and the voices of many friends. All gone now. All victims of the Nazi Holocaust. The walls she stared at were no longer home.

Corrie was left with the horrible memories of a concentration camp. She had seen the worst men can do to each other. She knew many would never recover from the scars left by that experience. Standing alone in the night, Corrie wondered what the future might hold.

Then suddenly a church began to play its familiar chimes. Corrie walked out into the street and paused to look up at the cathedral silhouetted against a black sky and framed by countless twinkling stars.

She remembered the words of Jesus, "Lo, I am with you alway, even unto the end of the world." Matthew 28:20.

Corrie stood there a long time, until the chimes played again. This time "A Mighty Fortress Is Our God" rang out in the night. Yes, Corrie realized, I do have a home in the everlasting arms of my heavenly Father. I have security. And there in the street she thanked the Lord for reminding her of His grace.

Corrie would not be trapped by old scars. Now she was free.

Each of us can be free of the past, each of us can renew our minds, when we truly see that we are accepted in the Beloved. And remember, the Beloved Son is also the Wounded Healer. And He always will be a Wounded Healer.

After Christ's resurrection, He appeared to His disciples in the upper room. Jesus possessed a new, glorified body. He had already appeared in heaven before His Father. And yet this resurrected Lord showed the disciples hands still deeply scarred—and a large wound on His side.

A glorified, risen Saviour—still bearing scars. Why?

Because what happened at Calvary will never be forgotten. I believe that Christ will always bear the scar of the trauma of the cross. The memory of that ordeal will stay with Him throughout eternity.

But the scars are not ugly. In heaven we won't turn our faces away from them. No. They speak of Christ's great sacrifice for mankind. They eloquently symbolize the most beautiful act of love this universe has ever known.

We, too, can't just erase our scars or pretend that they never happened. But God's love can transform them. His grace can fashion a new identity out of old wounds. The past may have been dark, but we can hear His song ringing out in the night. His assurance will come. And we can know that, today, right now, we do have a home in the everlasting arms.

Formula for Two

Happy marriage is not a glamorous package that the partners discover in the huge pile of wedding gifts. It is not something made and stored in heaven ready to be handed out to any two applicants. Rather, it is a do-it-yourself project. It has been suggested that it is like one of those kits which comes knocked down for putting together. It will take some gluing. Some sanding of rough spots. Hammering a bit. Filing down the scratches. Planing, carving, bending, varnishing—and then backing off to take a look. Dusting and waxing and polishing until at last you recognize it as a dream fulfilled.

What is it that makes a house a home? What is it that transforms a collection of people into a happy family? What is it that makes home a father's kingdom where the wife is queen, every daughter a princess, every son an heir—and where Christ reigns over all? Evidently the family tie is the closest, the most tender and sacred on earth. Listen!

> Love is not passion, love is not pride;
> Love is a journeying side by side.
> Not of the breezes, nor of the gale—
> Love is the steady set of the sail.

> Deeper than ecstasy, sweeter than light,
> Born in the sunshine, born in the night,
> Flaming in victory, strongest in loss,
> Love is a sacrament made for a cross.

I think right here you want me to share with you the Scripture formula for true love. It is not only a *formula for two,* but a formula for getting along with people anywhere. For in every relationship in life it's people that make the problem. Listen to 1 Corinthians 13:4-7, reading from the New English Bible:

"Love is patient; love is kind and envies no one. Love is never boastful, nor conceited, nor rude; never selfish, not quick to take offence. Love keeps no score of wrongs; does not gloat over other men's sins, but delights in the truth. There is nothing love cannot face; there is no limit to its faith, its hope, and its endurance."

There you have it! God's *formula for two.* Read it again and again. Evidently we are here dealing with a dimension in human relationships that has been little understood. For here is emphasized so precisely the value of the individual—the other individual. So often it has been overlooked. And, as a result, the partner's sense of security has been threatened.

I am not talking about a bank account. I am talking about security in the other's affections. For I have discovered that a sense of security and a feeling of personal worth are as important to a man or a woman as life and health. Nothing can so quickly encourage happiness in marriage as to build in your mate a sense of security in your affection, the feeling of being valued and loved and needed. Without such a foundation happiness will have a very short life.

Check yourself by the divine formula—if you dare. I

promise you, the revelation may be disturbing. At least, I found it so. Are you patient? Are you kind? Are you boastful and conceited, sometimes rude? Are you selfish and sensitive, quick to take offense? And tell me, do you keep a score of wrongs, slights, and injustices that come your way? Are you quick to watch out for your rights, careful to see that they are recognized by others?

Bruce Barton tells a little-known story from the experience of Abraham Lincoln. In the early months of the Civil War, Lincoln and a member of his cabinet went to call on General McClellan. Official etiquette prescribes that the President shall not call upon a private citizen. But the times were too tense for protocol. Lincoln needed firsthand information, and McClellan was the only man in Washington who could give it.

The General was not at home, and the two men waited in his parlor for an hour. Finally they heard him at the door and supposed that he would speak to them immediately. But without a word he hurried upstairs. They waited another thirty minutes. Finally Lincoln asked one of the servants to remind the General that they were still waiting. After a few moments the servant returned and told them, with obvious embarrassment, that McClellan had said he was too tired to see the President. In fact, he had already undressed and gone to bed.

When the two men were outside the house, the cabinet member exploded in anger. Should not Lincoln instantly oust McClellan from command? But the President laid his hand quietly on the other man's shoulder. "Don't take it so hard," he said. "I'll hold McClellan's horse, if he will only bring us victories."

Why was Lincoln willing to accept this insult to his dignity? There was a great purpose in his heart to win the war and to free a race. That was his passion. His pride, his position, his dignity, his rights took second place.

That's how the formula works. That's how it works in public life. That's how it works in the home. "Love seeketh not her own." The destiny of the home, the future of two souls, the happiness of our mates—these come first. Our own rights, our dignity, the respect due us—these come second. Strangely enough, happiness can more easily find us when we stand second in line.

I have discovered, too often the hard way, that the secret of lasting marriage is made up of little things—little unselfish acts, little words, little courtesies, little attentions. Why is it that we have kind words for others through the day, but when we cross the threshold of our own homes there is a tendency to let down? Why—when we love our own the best?

> We have careful thoughts for the stranger,
>   Sweet smiles for the sometime guest,
> But oft for our own, the bitter tone,
>   Though we love our own the best.
>   —Margaret Sangster

The threshold of home can be a lift instead of a letdown. We need not leave tact and human kindness on the office desk. You love your family deeply. But do they know it? Do we take too much for granted?

Christianity in the home, you see, includes appreciation and kindness and culture and simple courtesy, as well as uprightness of character. Bluntness, painful frankness, the brand of honesty that always says what it thinks, no matter how unkind—these are not virtues, but faults. They do not belong in the home. In fact, they do not belong in any relationship.

The four walls of home were meant to enclose happiness, not to shut it out. Home should be more than a temporary shelter for wounded sensitivities and broken hearts. And it can be. When Christ is in the home, it will be a place where we give our own the best, where the simple attentions and courtesies of courtship come as naturally as the day they were born.

A choice story that my wife Nellie discovered in her reading and which I have told around the world is that of a couple about to celebrate their golden wedding anniversary. (And incidentally, did you know that, even with the eroding elements of this twentieth century, one fifth of our marriages last more than fifty years?) In this instance a local newspaper sent out a reporter for an interview, and the husband was at home.

"What is your recipe for a long, happy marriage?" the reporter asked.

"Well, I'll tell you, young fellow," the old gentleman said slowly. "I was an orphan, and I always had to work pretty hard for my board and keep. I never even looked at a girl until I was grown. Sarah was the first one I ever kept company with. When she maneuvered me into proposing, I was scared stiff. But after the wedding her pa took me aside and handed me a little package. 'Here is all you really need to know,' he said. And this is what was in the package."

He reached for a large gold watch in his pocket, opened it, and handed it to the reporter. Across the face of the watch, where he could see it a dozen times a day, were the words: *"Say something nice to Sarah."*

Too simple to work, you say? But it did. Just remember that great happiness is purchased by small, inexpensive tokens. Thoughts of appreciation pay. Criticism does not. Understanding, tender affection, freely expressed—these build a happy relationship.

But sometimes kindness and appreciation are pushed aside and forgotten. Sometimes, I have painfully discovered, there has to be some mending done, some verbal repairing, some changing of heart, some assuming of personal blame. Every marital raft fit to face the gale will have to have the ropes tied a little tighter now and then before risking the rapids.

High on the list of happy marriages that I have known about is that of Bob and Helen. Dr. Charles Shedd recalls the details.

Bob was a pusher, and she was retiring. He was the life of a party; she stayed in the shadows. Yet they seemed perfectly mated. You would see them holding hands and exchanging a sly smile as if they were reading some silent message between them.

One night they gave a dinner party. Several times Bob went to the kitchen and offered to help. Finally she let him pour the water. And then, when all was ready, he served her first! I don't know what book of etiquette he had been reading. But she sat there beaming, as if it was supposed to be that way.

The whole dinner was a thing of beauty. Several times during the course of the conversation he asked her opinion on some subject—and even listened while she expressed it.

After dinner a guest took Bob aside and asked him the secret of his happy marriage.

"I tell you," he said, "it hasn't always been this way. The first couple of years of our marriage were pretty rough, until we were ready to call it quits. Then one day we decided to make a list of all the things we didn't like about each other. The lists were pretty long, but Helen gave me hers and I gave her mine. It was pretty rough reading. Some of the things we had never said out loud or shared in any way.

"Then we did what sounds like a foolish thing. We went out to the backyard to the ash can and burned those lists, watched them go up in smoke, while we put our arms around each other for the first time in months. Then we went back into the house, and we each made a list of all the good things we could dig up about each other. This took a little time. It was hard, because we were pretty down on our marriage. But we kept at it.

"Then we did another thing that might look silly to you. Come on back to the bedroom and I'll show you." He led his friend to the neat, attractive bedroom. And there at the focal point on the wall, in two maple frames, were two scratchy lists.

"If we have any secret, it is this," Bob confided. He told how he had memorized his list while driving to work, how he kept repeating it every day. And he said, "Now I think she is the most wonderful person in the world. And I guess she feels the same about me. That's all."

That's all? But it goes to the heart of a great marriage—this canceling out the bad and building up the good. Theirs was homemade heaven! With two scratchy lists on the wall!

Remember what the apostle Paul says? "Love keeps no score of wrongs." Take them out to the ash can—literally. Burn them up!

Friend, your relationship may need mending. If it does, remember that the strong threads of kindness and appreciation are the most lasting material you can use.

Every home needs mending. Every home has misunderstandings. Every home has disagreements. But the longer I live and the more people I meet, the more I realize that the most delicate care must be used in settling these conflicts. For differences of opinion, in the loaded, dangerous atmosphere of criticism and blame, are highly explosive.

Here is good counsel for your home and mine. Never quarrel at breakfast. Many a husband has torn out of the driveway, spinning gravel on his way to a collision, after a breakfast-table quarrel. And many a wife has spent her day in regret. Now follow through. Never quarrel when he comes home from work. A husband can stand almost anything at work if he has a happy home. Never let him come home to a nagging wife. And then, never quarrel after lights are out. It spoils the day.

In fact, my counsel would be simply, Never quarrel! There are no good quarrels. Let the steam off some other way. Quarrels never clear the air—they only poison it. Quarrels only scar. Current books to the contrary, a fight is a fight, whether the weapons used are fists or adjectives. Word wounds are often worse than those made by clubs.

Have you read "The First Settler's Story" recently? That time-worn tale is one of pathos, but it contains a lot of wise counsel for married hearts. You remember the young settler came home tired after a long day's work. For some reason, without his wife's knowing it, the cows had escaped. And he blamed her for it. "You had nothing else to do!" he said. "You could at least have watched the cows!"

Immediately he regretted his bitter words. But the damage was done. He felt led to beg her forgiveness that night, but his pride stood in the way. The next morning he was in a hurry and left reconciliation for another time.

Late in the afternoon he saw a storm coming up and headed for home. The cabin was empty. But there on the table was a note. "The cows have gone again," it said. "I'm sorry. I tried to keep them in. Please have kind words for me when you come home. I have gone to find the cows."

His wife? Out in that storm? He hurried after her, caring nothing now about the cows. She had not realized the severity of the storm that now broke in all its fury. While lightning tore across the sky, ripping it into deafening crashes of thunder that released a blinding hail, he searched frantically for his dear one. All night he combed the hills and valleys. Then with the morning sun he returned to the cabin, only to find her limp body lying not far from where he had killed her with his tongue. It was too late—*too late for words!*

> If I had known in the morning
> How wearily all the day
>   The words unkind
>   Would trouble my mind
> I said when you went away,
> I had been more careful, darling,
>   Nor given you needless pain;
> But we vex our own
> With look and tone
>   We might never take back again.
>
> For though in the quiet evening
> You may give me the kiss of peace,
>   Yet it might be
>   That never for me
> The pain of the heart should cease.
> How many go forth in the morning
>   That never come home at night,
> And hearts have broken
> For harsh words spoken
>   That sorrow can ne'er set right. . . .

> "Oh, lips with the curve impatient,
>   And brow with that look of scorn,
> 'Twere a cruel fate
> Were the night too late
>   To undo the work of the morn."
> —Margaret Sangster

In any home, I say, there will be differences of opinion that need to be discussed. It is a good rule never to go to sleep at night until misunderstandings have been cleared up, if there have been any. The apostle Paul says, "Never go to bed angry—don't give the devil that sort of foothold." Ephesians 4:26, 27, Phillips.

I believe you will regret any deviation from this plan. Differences are best approached in the quiet, uncharged atmosphere of tenderness and understanding, with forgiveness freely granted. For misunderstandings, if not cleared up promptly, become set in the mind as attitudes and can eventually ruin a marriage.

And now I want to ask you a question. You love your wife. You love your husband. But have you ever thought of him or her as your best friend? Stop just here for a moment and think it through. Your best friend. Basically, husband and wife are friends. Wouldn't this idea relax many a strained relationship?

Friends. Don't friends do things together? Don't friends share things together? Are you letting your marriage become only an assumed responsibility, rather than a spontaneous friendship? Someone has said that love is friendship set to music. Is it that way with you? Or are you trying to keep the love when the friendship has long been lost? Are you drinking from the brazen cups of duty while you could be drinking from the golden chalices of friendship?

Do things together. And it doesn't stop with husband and wife. Every child that enters the home needs attention. He needs *two* dedicated parents. He needs their time. He needs the sacrifice of selfish plans. Happy families play together, work together, explore life together, build a boat together—even if it leaks. Just ask my boys and my daughter Connie about the boat that leaked. Go camping together. It doesn't matter so much what you do. But do it together. Memory tells me I should have done it more.

And another secret. When couples, and families, learn to pray together, they will have discovered an important factor in preventing marital difficulties. Family prayer was once an established institution. When it declined, up went home problems and divorce. The number of people who go on week after week, month after month, year after year, without family devotions, is simply appalling—many of them professed Christians.

What about prayer in *your* home? God said through Jeremiah, "My people have forgotten me days without number." Jeremiah 2:32. Makes one think, doesn't it?

In one home where a Christian mother had passed away, the little girl told a stranger in awed and frightened tones, "We haven't had prayer in our house since Mother died, and *nothing has happened yet!*"

What a poor, limited conception of what prayer really means! Are our children being taught that prayer is merely a fire escape? No, nothing had happened in that home. Nothing but slow, imperceptible decay.

God isn't going to strike us dead. He loves us too much for that. There probably won't be any serious calamity aside from spiritual disintegration. And thus gradually we lose out just when we think we are strongest.

Worship in the home, making the home Christ-centered, can be a most happy experience in the lives of our children. They need not be made to feel that prayer time is an unwelcome duty or a burden.

A word just here. The devotional program of one home may not be best for another. The schedule of family devotions will need to be tailored to the needs of your home. This is what I mean. The ideal, it would seem, would be to gather the family together for prayers both morning and evening. But suppose that you have tried it. It worked fine in the morning. But when you attempted it after the evening meal, the children complained, the phone rang constantly, and everybody had to wait. Tableclearing, dishes, and homework were all delayed. Everybody went to bed tense and cross. But you had had your family devotions!

That, for your home, may not be the best plan. Then you might try continuing with the family group together for morning worship. But at bedtime let each parent spend time individually with each child—talking over any problems, praying together. Let each child look forward to this time with Father and with Mother that is completely his own. In my own home we followed the first plan as our two older boys were growing up. Now, with the younger son and my daughter, we find the second plan happier. There is a right way, a best way, for your home. Find it—and then follow it consistently.

No amount of family devotion, of course, can take the place of your own time alone with God. But even here there is a right way—a way that will help, not prejudice, the lives that you touch. In one home the father rose early each morning for meditation and prayer alone in his den. His small daughter followed him one morning, but was told to "get out of here." She asked her mother what daddy was doing. And mother said,

"He's trying to learn to love the people downtown."

Love the people downtown? And lose one's own? Fortunately that father saw his mistake, and soon it was not unusual for one of the children to join him in his morning prayer.

Is it possible to overestimate the saving influence of a Christian home? Children may wander in the wilderness for a while during the disturbing upheaval of adolescence. But the memory of consistent, honest dedication in the home will never be erased. God said through Isaiah, "I will contend with him that contendeth with thee, and I will save thy children." Isaiah 49:25.

Trouble With the Personnel

A young man asked a physician for the hand of his daughter in marriage. The doctor refused. It was quite a setback, but the young suitor gathered courage to ask, "Why can I not marry your daughter? I love her."

The doctor replied, "I think you do."

"I can support her."

"I suppose you can."

"Then why can't I marry her?"

To this the doctor answered, "My daughter has a miserable disposition. Nobody could live with her and be happy."

The young man gallantly replied, "But there is always the grace of God."

The doctor smiled understandingly. "When you are as old as I am, young man, you will realize that the grace of God can live with some people that you can't live with!"

The trouble with marriage is not with the institution. It's with the personnel. The trouble is with people. It's people that need to be changed. Unhappy couples don't dislike marriage. They dislike each other. The challenge in marriage is not only in *finding* the right person, but *being* the right person. Many a wife has thought she needed a new husband, only to realize that her husband needed a new wife.

TROUBLE WITH THE PERSONNEL 29

Too many marriages have gone on the rocks because one partner entered the contract secretly planning to change the other. And it doesn't usually work that way. If a bus says "Cincinnati," that is likely where it is going. You can't count on its changing destinations after you board it. It's the same with husbands and wives.

Glenn Clark, popular author and publisher, has listed some beatitudes of a happy marriage. One of them is this: "Blessed are the married ones who strive first of all to make their mates *happy* rather than *good*."

The trouble is that so many of us feel it is our duty to make our mates good—and we sometimes make everyone concerned unhappy in the process. I have been guilty. But I have discovered that if we persevere in trying to make our mates happy, we more easily succeed in the other objective.

We are talking here about sound principles of interpersonal relationship. To be sure, they are especially applicable in the unique relationships of marriage where a home must survive or perish. But the same foundation principles will succeed in the relations of friend with friend, doctor with patient, employer with employee. And surprisingly enough, we often discover that the difficulty is not *between* two people, but *within* two people, *within* the individual. Changing your own heart, you see, is likely to be the surest and fastest way to change the heart of your mate.

Why do we continue to struggle with the simplest lessons in personal relations when we ought to be taking an advanced course? One couple visited a marriage counselor after nineteen years of marriage. The counselor told them, "You have not had nineteen years of experience in marriage. You have simply lived the first year nineteen times."

The secrets of marital success are not elusive. I feel strongly that if we would put the hard work and ingenuity into our homes that we put into our jobs, we would succeed.

Tact and insight. These are invaluable in the office environment. They are equally indispensable at home. Human nature does not respond charitably to bluntness. Tact, you see, is saying the right thing, the right kind of thing, at the right time, in the right way. Tact involves not only words, but the tone of voice, the mood, the atmosphere, the motive. And insight is the willingness to understand another's point of view—with the possibility that it may be right. Together they are the healing therapy that reaches into a wounded heart and avoids a crisis. Without tact and insight, marriage too often becomes a savage contest in which each partner tries to wound more deeply than the other.

Why should we be so blind to the fact that we have faults too? The most ideal person has faults. And marriage in itself does not eliminate them. But we get in a hurry. We expect marriage to solve automatically and instantly all the problems we had before marriage.

A college girl knows that it takes time to adjust to a new roommate. A violinist knows that he will not be a professional when first he picks up the instrument. But we expect marriage to be different. We may be unhappy single. We may be miserable in school. We may be in conflict with our parents. But we expect marriage to change us miraculously and instantaneously into ecstatically happy persons. And it doesn't work that way.

It is when we begin to accept life as it is, and our mates as they are, that we begin to move toward a happy home.

A young wife, married about three years, breezed into her pastor's office, tossed her coat over a chair, and exploded, "Honestly, Bill is the most ornery, stubborn, independent, obstinate—ooooh! But you know what? I'm learning to live with him! Now how do you like that!" And then she added, "He's adorable! I would never have believed it possible that I could be so extremely exasperated with a man yet love him so dearly." And she was gone.

Of course, if you are normal, you have probably experienced some degree of marital tension. There are those who say they have never quarreled. That may be true. Or it may be that they are simply giving their quarrels another label. One husband said, "We've never had an argument in thirty years of married life. However, we have engaged in serious discussions which the neighbors heard a block away."

Every home, I say, has some problems. Some homes more than others. A marriage counselor asked one young couple, "What do you have in common?"

The wife replied, "One thing. Neither of us can stand the other."

John Milton, the unhappily married poet, once heard his wife referred to as a rose. He remarked, "I am no judge of flowers. But it may be true, for I feel the thorns daily." And John Wesley's wife used to sit in City Road Chapel and make faces at him while he preached!

Let me repeat again, there are no good quarrels. It is unfortunate that those who write the marriage manuals often think it necessary to include a chapter on how to quarrel. Don't we agree that quarrels only weaken the relationship, each encounter leaving it less secure?

There was the man who said, "Oh, she would never leave me."

"Don't be too sure," said the minister to whom the wife had already come in great distress.

And the man said, "Why, she can't do that to me. What would I do without her?"

The minister asked quietly, "Did you ever tell her that?"

"No," the man admitted. "I don't like such talk."

When it was suggested that he take home some flowers and recourt the woman of his choice, this huge, clumsy-looking fellow exclaimed, "Now wouldn't I look fine luggin' home flowers? I'd feel like a fool." Just the same, he did it. And it broke the growing coolness, stimulated the basic strong original affection between them.

Too simple to work, you say? Don't you believe it. Flowers may not always be the answer. But a lack of appreciation in small things can grow until it becomes a great divisive factor.

Do you take your mate for granted? Or are you attempting, by little acts of thoughtfulness, coupled with the appropriate words, to protect your marriage against deterioration? Is your companion secure in your affection? Does she know, does he know, that no attack from without can shake the ship of matrimony? Do the children know it?

One expert has said, "The most important thing a father can do for his children is to love their mother." How quickly little children are unsettled by dissension in the home! Only when they know that nothing can crack the rock of their domestic tranquillity will they be content.

Do you remember—even in moments of crisis—that your wife is a person—your children are persons? Do you remember their need for a sense of security and a feeling of personal worth? Have you made a determined effort to understand those needs? For tragedy sets in, homes begin to disintegrate, when we do not understand. It starts with little neglects, little misunderstandings, little selfish attitudes—until finally there is constant bulldozing and belittling until the last spark of identity is killed and the heart is drained of its desire to continue!

Nagging, that demonic tactical maneuver in a psychological battle, is often the culprit. Said the wise man, "A continual dripping on a rainy day and a contentious woman are alike." Proverbs 27:15, RSV.

And one modern authority has written, "Most cases of emotionally induced illness are the result of a monotonous drip, drip of . . . unpleasant emotions, the everyday run of anxieties, fears, discouragements and longings."—Dr. John Schindler, *How to Live 365 Days a Year,* p. 13.

Who can take the drip-of-the-faucet treatment for long—especially when it comes from someone you love?

How can the rift be healed? How can the gulf be bridged? Communication. That is the answer. Talking it over is a cornerstone in building a successful marriage. There should be a willingness to talk at all times. Many a misunderstanding could be healed in minutes if both partners would calmly evaluate it. There is nothing in all of marriage more destructive than the presence of a silent rift.

One wife said, "You know how you feel when the phone rings and nobody answers? That is how I feel."

There is a lifetime of communication ahead of each of us. Wouldn't it be wise to learn the art better? The heart of marriage is its communication system. Communication breakdown is a chief source of trouble in all human relationships—especially in the intimate and continuing relationship of marriage.

It is impossible not to communicate. If we do not communicate with words, we will be communicating by our silence. And our silence may be as easily misunderstood as our words.

The communication in marriage is not the same as communication of courtship. The excitement of exploring each other's lives begins to disappear. The girl who was once so glamorous is now washing dishes. The ability to communicate now, in changing circumstances, may determine whether the marriage survives or not.

Honesty at this point is all-important. Playing games will not do. Wearing masks will not do. Masks cannot communicate. Only people can communicate. And the intimate ties of marriage are never strengthened by pretense.

Those who communicate, in any area of life, face one baffling problem: *Is anyone listening?* Do you hear what your wife says? Or is your mind taking a meaningful excursion elsewhere? It is estimated that we spend about 70 percent of our waking hours in communication of some kind—speaking, listening, reading, or writing. Evidently listening is mighty important.

Marriage, unfortunately, provides no guarantee that the partners will listen to each other or try to understand each other. Too often when one is speaking, the other is really not present. He is running errands in his mind. The happy lesson to be learned is that love listens. It is only as love listens that love can understand. Listening will do what words cannot. Did you ever try to find the right words to let someone know his opinions are important to you? Listening will do it as if by magic.

Robert Soudek wrote of John F. Kennedy, "He made you think he had nothing else to do except ask you questions and listen—with extraordinary concentration—to your answers."

Sometimes, in the marital relationship, you get a

busy signal. If a husband has been barraged with messages all day, he may, without ever knowing it, tune out his wife just as he would a television set. One wife said, "My husband can have the TV and the radio on at the same time, listening to two different games at once. The kids can pester him endlessly with interruptions, yet he can tell you the progress of either game whenever you ask. This is the same guy who can sit at the supper table without any distractions whatever and not hear a word I say."

Evidently we *choose* to listen.

Human nature is so persistent. Speaking, you see, is a way of asserting one's self. Listening is not. That's why it is easier to speak than to listen. This inward need for self-assertion is manifested in many ways. For instance, there is the chronic interrupter who constantly attempts to take the ball. There is the one who breaks into the conversation with "that reminds me" and diverts the topic of discussion into his own channel. Then there is the one who breaks in with "I know just what you are going to say," and thereby robs the speaker of any opportunity whatever for unique expression. Such a listener listens with only one thought in mind—"Where do I come in?"

Then there is the man who is always right. His mind is already closed. Lucy, of *Peanuts* fame, says, "I have a new ambition. When I get big, I'd like to be a baseball umpire." Charlie Brown asks, "What in the world makes you think you could be a good baseball umpire?" With head high, Lucy replies, "Because I'm always right!"

Excessive talking, which may or may not be compulsive, is another way to avoid listening. Sometimes it is an attempt to divert the conversation from an unwelcome subject. Who has not seen it?

One of the most frequent problems in marriage is the husband who will not listen. But is the conversation worth listening to? The wife should make sure it is. Small talk may seem entirely too insignificant in contrast with the big ideas that have filled the husband's office hours.

Marriage partners who will not listen are already experiencing a separation of interests. For where there is no dialogue, there is emotional divorce. Would it be too strong to suggest that whenever one mate stops listening to the other, he is guilty of a sort of infidelity? It is in attentive and understanding listening that marriage matures.

Talk is absolutely essential in marriage. It's married strangers who quarrel most readily. Silence may be golden—sometimes. But silence can also kill. Buttoned-up lips too often indicate an unsteady heart. Without verbal spillways the tension inside becomes too great, and tragedy can result. The very first barrier to communication should be a danger signal.

One of the most frequent circuit jammers in the marital communication system is the perfectionist within us. The perfectionist is never on a level with his mate. He has to prove everything he says. Even when he is wrong he is right. He may make a good proofreader, but can you think of a more impossible person to live with? Successful marriage partners early learn to communicate as imperfectionists. The apostle John says, "If we say that we have no sin, we deceive ourselves." 1 John 1:8.

I have learned to my chagrin that good communication is deeply involved in semantics.

You know, of course, what a particular word means to you. But what does it mean to your mate? Brittle relationships can be broken by a troublesome word. Is it asking too much for a husband, instead of resorting to stupid adjectives, to say gently, "Why, yes, I can *see* how *anyone* would misunderstand. But this is what I meant."

When a husband and wife get into heated debate, there is always the temptation to forsake the issue and attack the person. There is a Latin term for it—*ad hominem,* meaning "to the man." There are lawyers who, finding themselves without a case, resort to personal attacks. But let's keep the *ad hominems* out of marriage. It's the personal arrows that fly straightest to the mark and leave the deepest scars.

Many a marital rift can be quickly healed by calmly, quietly, and understandingly talking it over. But remember. A sense of security and a feeling of personal worth—these are the basis for opening doors. There can be no useful communication without them. Talking things over without first reestablishing this interrupted undercurrent of confidence in each other's affections is often useless. Communication without first reaffirming one's affection may only degenerate into defense and justification and accusation. Only when love is first solidly reanchored can there be a basis for understanding.

Tell me, Is your antenna so directed that your companion can receive the message? Is yours a relaxed attitude—an environment that encourages talking it over? There may be a torrent of words. But if there is not an attitude of confidence and respect and willingness to listen to the other side with the possibility that it may even be the right side, there is no real communication.

"I love you." These are hard words to say in a moment of tension and misunderstanding. But we need to say them. And we may need to add three words even harder to say—"I was wrong." There are times when a heart cannot be healed without those words. No wonder that the apostle James wrote, "Confess your faults one to another, and pray one for another, that ye may be healed." James 5:16.

You ask, "What does confession have to do with healing?"

Simply this. We are fast learning that fear, anger, resentment, and bitterness not only lay the groundwork for divorce, but actually poison the body system. Fussing one's way to the divorce court may lead also to the hospital. The body is not made for hate. Body, mind, and soul are made for happiness.

We need to remember that a marital rift, with the scars it has left on mind and body, is healed more easily with words of honest confession than with gifts. In fact, one of the serious delusions of our day is the notion that hearts can be mended with material things. We seem to be caught up in a feverish rush to acquire more and more in the elusive hope of finding happiness and understanding therein.

A few years ago a huge floor-covering corporation featured an ad with all the color and modern appeal of design. Across the ad in striking, bold letters were these words: "Lay linoleum and have a happy home!"

Do you see? Too often when there is home trouble, we think we can heal it if we *lay linoleum*. If there is quarreling or bickering, *lay linoleum*. If the children are wild and disobedient, *lay linoleum*. No. Laying linoleum—or wall-to-wall carpet, for that matter, installing a deepfreeze, or contracting for a second automobile—is not the secret of a lasting marriage.

Too many homes are trying to substitute things for words, responsibility for romance, tolerance for love— and hoping the world will never guess!

Dr. Louis Evans draws a fascinating lesson from the

story of ancient Israel. You can read it in 1 Kings 14. Solomon, in the days of his glory, had made "three hundred shields of beaten gold." 1 Kings 10:17.Then Solomon died, and the glory of the kingdom perished with him.

In the days of Rehoboam, son of Solomon, we read that Shishak, leader of the enemy hosts, "took away all the shields of gold which Solomon had made."

What should they do now? The glory had faded. But Rehoboam determined that the world should never know. He would keep up appearances. He gave the order to make replacement shields of brass that glittered as pure gold. With these they were to parade bravely and unfalteringly.

"In many a home," says Dr. Evans, "the golden shields of romance have been stolen; the thievery of time or drabness or selfishness or treason or coldness have walked away with the golden shields of romance and rich newness. Marriage is no longer a parade, it is a sullen march."—*Your Marriage—Duel or Duet?* p. 123.

How is it in your home, friend? Are you bravely parading with highly polished shields of brass, when they might have been—might still be—shields of pure gold?

What of those who watch the parade? Is your home a convincing demonstration of happiness wall to wall? Do friends and neighbors covet its secret?

And what of the children, the teenagers who are a part of that home? What does it look like from the inside? Gold? Or brass? Do they consider it the genuine thing? Or only a careless copy? Are they using it as a pattern for their own interpersonal relationships? Are they planning to borrow its blueprint for homes of their own? Or are they left to solve the teenage dilemma with shields of brass, a heritage of make-believe?

There is no more important question.

Your Irreplaceable Role

Remember Claude Monet—the revolutionary genius who taught the world to see in a totally different way? The play of light and color on his canvases revolutionized the art world. His exhibitions at first produced shock, outrage, and quiet awe. In time, the world would come to regard him as uniquely inspired. But Claude Monet's talented eye failed to see, really see, one critical thing: a girl named Camille. And she proved to be the one irreplaceable part of his inspiration.

In nineteenth-century Paris, the Academy of Fine Arts was all-powerful. For artists, the road to success lay through Academy teachers who taught painting in the approved style: correct, finished, and lifeless. Talented students might someday exhibit their works in the Academy Salon. Only there could a painter receive the attention of the critics and, eventually, admission to the Academy.

Claude Monet, however, just couldn't bring himself to take that road. What was the point of merely copying the same old scenes in a certain style? Monet had to paint what his own eye saw, directly from nature. He wanted to capture the liveliness of things—the interaction of light, color, and shape in one momentary impression.

YOUR IRREPLACEABLE ROLE 41

Monet's parents wanted to help their son become a great painter. But they insisted that he take the respectable way toward a more prosperous art career. "You must study with the Academy of Fine Arts," they said, "or we will not support you."

This Monet could not do. So he struggled on alone, barely scraping together enough to live on, and painting, always painting. "I am the prisoner of my eye," he once said. His one unchanging goal would always be to represent truthfully his own vision of life and nature.

One of Monet's favorite subjects was Camille, a beautiful, graceful model. His admiration for her deepened into love, and they were married.

Monet had become a leader in the new art movement called Impressionism. But he could not sell his work. When he exhibited paintings in galleries, the crowds only laughed. The critics were sarcastic. "Even wallpaper . . . is more finished that THAT," one said. A newspaper cartoon pictured a policeman warning pregnant women to stay away from an Impressionist exhibition—the shock would be too great.

Monet and Camille endured much privation. The struggle to get enough food and find a place to stay seemed endless. But Camille never complained. She believed in her husband's dream.

And through worry, disappointment, and suffering, Monet continued to produce his bright, lively canvases. Camille had become central to his art. She appears in many of his paintings—in the fields, tall and stately—in their gardens—on the beach—and with their son Jean. Her deep, dark eyes hint at both sorrow and a quiet determination.

But the strain of barely surviving took its toll. Camille's health was suffering. Monet became desperate. She just had to get better. But how? He couldn't bring himself to stop painting and find some respectable job. Monet felt terribly guilty, but his obsession drove him on.

After the birth of their second child, Camille's illness worsened. Now they knew she had tuberculosis. Monet continued to paint feverishly, hoping against hope for a breakthrough. Surely someone would recognize his work soon; his paintings would sell; they could settle into more comfortable surroundings, and all would be well.

But the breakthrough didn't come in time. In 1879 tuberculosis claimed Camille's life. Monet still had a studio full of unsold paintings. Camille had never complained; she had always supported her husband in his work. But now she was gone.

And something else was lost too, though Monet didn't realize it at first. As one biographer put it, "With Camille's death, his wonderful eye lost its most powerful creative force." All the warmth, the humanity, and the deep feeling in his pictures had come, indirectly, from her.

A few years later the breakthrough finally arrived. The public had begun to accept Impressionism. Monet's paintings started to sell. His reputation grew. Finally Monet was making it as an artist—but without Camille. Monet was tortured by this thought: Could even the struggle for true art be worth the life of such a woman?

Monet was selling his older paintings, but he had difficulty with new work. He wrote, "I have scraped off all my latest canvases. I suffer anguish." And later in another location he said, "I've destroyed six [canvases] since coming here. I've done only one that pleases me. I'm tired of it all."

Monet had only to paint what he pleased, and it would sell for any price he demanded. But he found himself increasingly bitter and restless. "I work hard," he wrote, "and make myself ill with wretchedness: I'm horribly worried by everything I do."

Monet had lost the one irreplaceable part of his inspiration. He had reason to be bitter, but perhaps he also had reason to reconsider. Monet had sacrificed his wife for his art, and then discovered that there could be little meaningful art without her. Monet's brilliant eye had not quite seen that Camille herself was his art and that making compromises to better care for her would have better preserved his art as well.

His admirable pursuit of excellence in art had not included a drive to be excellent at home—at the root of his inspiration.

Many of us have a similar problem. It is not always easy to balance the demands of our mission, our profession, with the needs of our home. We don't always see clearly what is truly irreplaceable. Tom was fortunate enough to make that discovery before it was too late.

Tom worked as a television technician. He was often called on to assist in the taping of special events. Tom was proud of his work; he understood the intricacies of television electronics well and had developed a special talent for troubleshooting during taping sessions.

One year Tom's union and the company he worked for couldn't settle on a contract. The union called a strike. Tom, along with the rest of his crew, walked off the job.

Tom didn't like the idea of just quitting. He felt uneasy sitting around the house. But he felt sure the company would settle on a contract quickly. After all, how could they get along without him and his crew? After years of experience, Tom had learned almost every detail involved in the production of a television program. Who else could they get with his expertise?

The strike, however, dragged on. The company didn't seem that desperate to compromise. And then Tom learned that he had been replaced. That was quite a blow—someone else filling his role. And what was worse, the company continued producing programs just as before. Tom had become dispensable.

His spirits plummeted. If he could be replaced so easily, how much did his life mean—what purpose could he really have? He wandered about the house aimlessly. But during this time of depression, Tom's family rallied around him. They comforted and encouraged him.

It was then that he began seeing himself in a new light. He looked again at those who depended on him day by day—his wife and children. And it dawned on Tom that there was one role in life no one but he could fulfill. There was one place where he would always be irreplaceable: in his family.

If Tom, the husband and father, went out on strike, no replacement would ever be found. No one else could have the same nurturing relationships he enjoyed with his wife and children.

Tom eventually went back to work and continued a productive career in television. But he no longer depended on his position for security. He understood where he was truly irreplaceable.

Have you made that discovery? Are you committed to fulfilling your one irreplaceable role? Or does your career crowd out time with the family? Does the pursuit of a promotion take priority over caring for your wife or husband?

Oh, I know we all give lip service to the idea that our families are most important. That's easy to SAY. But ask yourself this: When a decision has to be made between a demand at work and a need at home, how often do you choose the latter? Do you ever cancel appointments because you need to spend time with the family?

Probably not very often. Believe me, I know. We ministers are often the worst offenders—so busy trying to save the world that we neglect those closest to us.

The God of the Bible, however, has a different view of the matter. He values most what we often pass over. God made that point beautifully in a little book called Ruth. At the beginning of this Old Testament story we find three widows trudging down the long road from Moab to Judah. They are Naomi and her two daughters-in-law, Ruth and Orpah. A famine has been ravaging Moab. And Naomi has decided to go back to Judah, where food is more plentiful.

But as she walks on the dusty road, Naomi begins to think. Ruth and Orpah, both Moabites, will never be able to marry in Judah. As foreigners they will never be fully accepted. The girls would be better off staying in Moab. At least among their own people they *have* a chance of raising a family.

So Naomi stops and tells them, "Go back, each of you, to your mother's home. May the Lord show kindness to you."

But Ruth and Orpah reply, "We will go back with you to your people." After all, they are all the elderly woman has left. How could she survive alone?

Naomi, however, is insistent: "Return home, my daughters. Why would you come with me? Am I going to have any more sons, who could become your husbands?" Ruth 1:8-11, NIV.

Finally, Orpah embraces her mother-in-law and says a tearful farewell. But Ruth just can't tear herself away. Her devotion is too strong. This young girl makes a memorable promise: "Where you go I will go, and where you stay I will stay. Your people will be my people and your God my God. Where you die I will die." Ruth 1:16, 17, NIV.

Beautiful words. I can't imagine a more eloquent loyalty. Ruth understood her one irreplaceable role. She committed herself to the one family bond that remained.

Just two people, clinging to each other on the long road to Judah. You might think they would be rather insignificant in the vast sweep of biblical history. But God has emphasized their story. Ruth plays a special part in God's revelation. The book is actually His exclamation point at the end of another book called Judges.

Judges tells a pretty sorry story of Israel's repeated apostasies. At times, after some great deliverance, Israel would return to God, but soon they would be running after their neighbor's idols again. They could never decide altogether for the God of heaven.

Ruth is God's answer to that whole sad period. What a contrast this heathen girl provides to Israel's wishy-washy ways! God didn't need to preach a long sermon on loyalty after Israel's disappointing performance under the Judges. He just told this beautiful story of a girl and her mother-in-law.

This is what is really significant, God is saying. Kings and warriors may come and go, nations pass through prosperity and disaster, but this kind of loyal relationship is what matters in the end.

Ruth valued, above all, the role no one else could fill. And as a result she became one of God's great signs in history.

Your marriage can be another of God's beautiful signs. Paul tells us that the relationship between husband and wife is to reflect the relationship between

Christ and His church. The world must see, in the care, consideration, and respect of our home life, a picture of Christ's love for His people.

Nothing in our work, nothing in our careers, can provide that picture. All the marketing and advertising and salesmanship in the world can't provide it. Only the quality of our marriage relationships can say what God wants to say. We have an irreplaceable role to play.

God wants us to excel in our relationships at home. It is all part of our calling. It can't be separated from our mission in life. If we sacrifice our families for our mission, we will find, like the painter Monet, that we have no mission left.

Excellence in our family relationships—how few of us seek it. The pressures of the world constantly seek to divorce our calling at work from our calling at home.

Recently hundreds of academic professionals gathered to honor a man who had earned a Nobel prize in science. During the preliminary ceremonies his wife waited backstage with the wives of other men also to be honored. The wife of the Nobel prize winner didn't seem all that excited, and the other women asked her why.

"How can I be happy with a husband like that?" she asked, and went on to describe a rather pathetic home life.

Immediately the other women chimed in, "Why, that's my story, exactly." All had the same experience of neglect and abuse.

While cameras flashed on the stage and dignitaries gave admiring speeches, a very different story was unveiled backstage. Those closest to the honorees could only describe a common misery.

Excelling at work and failing at home. That's the status quo. And that's what the Word of God will not tolerate. Our mission in life is one seamless fabric. If we can't reflect Christ in our home life, what is the point of trying to promote Him at our jobs?

How are you doing in your irreplaceable role? When our world turns to ashes, we will not look back and say, "I wish I'd spent more time in the office." We will only look at the quality of our personal relationships. Our keenest joys and deepest regrets will all center on the people in our family circles we have touched for good or ill.

In this final moment with this little book *When Wounds Won't Heal*, will you be prepared to seek excellence where it really counts? Will you commit yourself to fulfill your irreplaceable role? I hope so.